SERMONS
FOR THE
CELEBRATION
OF THE
CHRISTIAN
YEAR

SERMONS FOR THE CELEBRATION OF THE CHRISTIAN YEAR

VANCE BARRON

ABINGDON   NASHVILLE

SERMONS FOR THE CELEBRATION
OF THE CHRISTIAN YEAR

Copyright © 1977 by Abingdon

All rights reserved.

Library of Congress Cataloging in Publication Data

BARRON, VANCE, 1916-
  Sermons for the celebration of the Christian year.
  1. Church year sermons. 2. Presbyterian Church—Sermons.
3. Sermons, American. I. Title.
BX9178.B375S47   252'.6   76-51402

ISBN 0-687-37775-7

Scripture quotations unless otherwise noted are from the Revised Standard Version of the Bible, copyrighted 1946, 1951, © 1971, 1973.

Poetry quotation on page 57 is taken from *Jesus Christ Superstar*, a rock opera by Andrew Lloyd Webber and Tim Rice, lyrics by Tim Rice, music by Andrew Lloyd Webber. © Copyright 1969 by Leeds Music Ltd., London, England. Sole selling agent Leeds Music Corporation, 445 Park Avenue, New York, New York, for North, South, and Central America. Used by permission. All rights reserved.

Stanza from poem "The House of Christmas" on page 32 is reprinted by permission of Dodd, Mead & Company, Inc., from *The Collected Poems of G. K. Chesterton*. Copyright 1932 by Dodd, Mead & Company, Inc. Copyright renewed 1959 by Oliver Chesterton. Permission for this same use is also granted by Miss D. E. Collins.

Scripture quotation noted NEB is from the New English Bible. © the Delegates of the Oxford University Press and the Syndics of the Cambridge University Press 1961, 1970. Reprinted by permission.

MANUFACTURED BY THE PARTHENON PRESS AT
NASHVILLE, TENNESSEE, UNITED STATES OF AMERICA

To the
congregation of University Presbyterian Church,
who have encouraged me greatly
as a preacher of the Word.

CONTENTS

PREFACE

All pastors and all congregations have some awareness of the Christian Year, and engage in the celebration of some of its principal festivals. There is no such thing as a "nonliturgical" church. There are churches—and pastors—whose liturgical practices are not as well thought out as they might be; but *wherever Christians assemble for corporate worship, there is liturgy.* Many of us could benefit from an increased consciousness of the Christian Year and from a more concerted effort to let it guide and support us as preachers and as leaders of corporate worship.

The Worshipbook, prepared by the major Presbyterian Churches in the U.S.A., contains this statement about the Christian Year: "As they worship, Christians are mindful of the mighty acts of God, especially as they are seen in the birth, the life, the death, and the resurrection of Jesus Christ. The pattern in which worshipers proceed from event to event and from remembrance to remembrance is called the Christian Year." In the same vein, James F. White suggests (in *New Forms of Worship* [Nashville: Abingdon Press, 1971] p. 41), that "a major portion of almost any service of Christian worship is a rehearsal of the community of faith's corporate memories of God's acts as narrated in Scripture."

These statements speak directly to both our worship and our preaching in the churches today. In recent years, many have commented on the sorry state of both worship and preaching, but not everyone has understood that these two things are related. But they are related! The renewal and reform of one can hardly take place without the renewal and reform of the other.

Some who recognize and deplore the state of worship in our churches find themselves at a loss, not knowing where to begin corrective measures. Others have embarked on efforts that have received the label of "experimental worship," and have found themselves less than happy with the results. It would appear that the renewal of worship requires something more than guitars, "now" songs, and dancers—although these may sometimes serve our purpose very well if we have a purpose that is theologically and ecclesiastically sound. But change merely for the sake of change usually leads us out of a bad situation into a worse one. To relate our worship and our preaching to the Christian Year, however, is to build on that which is proven and tested in Christian experience.

If we accept the definition of corporate worship suggested by *The Worshipbook* and James F. White in the preceding quotations, then it will appear that worship and preaching share a common purpose. What is the purpose of our preaching? If it is not that of remembering, rehearsing, celebrating (and encouraging) our response to the mighty acts of God, then I for one do not know what it is! And if it is that, then our preaching shares the overarching purpose of the whole worship service, as that purpose has been understood in the church catholic and expressed in the structure of the Christian Year.

Worship that follows the pattern of the Christian Year is almost assured of unity, direction, and wholeness—qualities so often lacking in much of our worship. The same can be said for preaching. If we have the courage to look back over the past few years of our preaching, we may find that it has been, in spite of its commendable quality on any given Sunday, an erratic wandering over the landscape of the faith. If we look at our record honestly, we may be forced to admit that our preaching over a period of time has been lacking in those qualities of unity, direction, and wholeness. Relating our preaching to the Christian Year could help us overcome such deficiencies. Further, it could provide us with that structure which enables the sermon to reinforce—and be reinforced by—other parts of the service.

For those who might fear that a following of the Christian Year would result in the loss of freedom and spontaneity in both worship and preaching, let me suggest that it is possible to make a full use of the Christian Year and at the same time retain considerable flexibility. The lectionary is the key to the year, but one may follow closely the progression and emphasis of the year without always using the lessons indicated in the lectionary for a particular Sunday. As interpreters of the Word, we all relate to the Scriptures in a very personal way. Our own acquaintance with the Scriptures may lead us to choose passages that serve the occasion better. This has certainly been my own experience, and you will note that for some of these sermons on the great Christian festivals I have used passages other than those suggested in the principal lectionaries. I do not feel that I have surrendered my freedom and flexibility by relating my preaching to the Christian Year. What I have gained is some discipline and direction, neither of which is unrelated to freedom. Preaching is not exempted from the law that applies in all other areas of life, namely, that we are most free when we are most disciplined by some guiding principle that we have internalized.

The sermons selected for publication in this small volume were first shared with the congregation of the University Presbyterian Church in Chapel Hill, North Carolina, in the course of that particular community of faith's movement through the cycle of the Christian Year. These sermons are not offered as models of preaching as such. Rather, they are offered as an example of one pastor's attempt to let his preaching follow the shape of the Christian Year. If they are helpful to others in their celebration of the great festivals of our faith, I shall be most grateful.

ADVENT

To Keep Hope Alive

I

The story of Noah and his ark is not something we grown-ups take very seriously. We tend to regard it as a story for children, and we have our children making replicas of the ark in Sunday school. But it is a very strange thing, really, that we should regard this as a children's story (which is to say a fairy tale), because it is a dark and frightening story. Furthermore, it is a story about ourselves and our world—a story that is quite modern.

II

This old man, Noah, heard a voice, or at least he thought that he did; and the speaker claimed to be God. The voice was telling him that the world was terribly wicked and corrupt and that God was getting ready to wash it out—quite literally. In a way, this was no surprise to Noah.

He knew how bad things were, and he had always assumed that God would judge the world; but of course that was the sort of thing one always envisioned for the distant future. But now? Right away? And him build an ark—a kind of floating zoo? He didn't know whether to laugh or to cry! Why, people would think he was crazy. *He* would think he was crazy! Anyway, how could he be sure that he *had* heard a voice?

So Noah had to decide, and it wasn't easy; but he decided that, crazy or not, he would obey God, and people would just have to think whatever they wanted to. So he started to build, and gradually the ark began to take shape out there on the hilltop behind his house. Crazy old Noah, building a boat on dry land miles and miles from any water that could float it! It really gave the neighbors a laugh! And it really was a crazy Rube Goldberg sort of contraption; but it was the best that he could manage, and it would have to do. After all, shipbuilding was not his thing.

But finally it was all finished—and then—guess what? Nothing happened! For a long time nothing happened at all, and the funny-looking ark just sat there in the dust. We can imagine the jokes that were passed around the neighborhood. And then one day there was the voice again, this time with the message that it was time to get on board. Noah looked up at the clear blue sky, shook his head, and started loading up. And before very long the sky darkened, the thunder clapped, and the rain began to fall—such a rain as people in those parts had never seen before!

It rained and it rained and it kept on raining, until finally everything was submerged, even the mountaintops. From the deck of the ark, which was bobbing around like a dry cork on the waves, Noah could see nothing but an endless stretch of water.

It must have been a depressing experience to look out on a drowned world, to know that there was no longer any life out there at all. And that aimless voyage must have seemed an eternity to Noah, although he had plenty of problems on board to occupy his mind. But then one day he went out on the top deck and looked around and thought that perhaps, just perhaps, the waters were receding a bit. The next day he looked again, and this time there could be no mistake about it. He looked off into the distance and was fairly certain that he saw the top of a mountain!

So he sent out a dove—and the dove was gone for several hours, and his hope was beating in his breast—but the dove returned—with nothing. He waited a week and released the dove again in the morning and again waited in hope. This time the dove was gone for a longer period of time, and Noah began to get excited. Then, just before sunset, the dove appeared, circled the ark, and came to rest on Noah's hand—and lo—in her mouth, a freshly plucked olive leaf!

Noah knew what that meant. It didn't mean that now they could leave that stinking mess on the ark—not right now. But it did mean that somewhere out there a world was being reborn, and that someday they could leave the ark and start a new life in a new world! So Noah lived in hope, a hope built on nothing more tangible than God's Word, a hope revived by a sign, a small sign, just a fresh leaf from an olive tree.

III

Such is the story in our Old Testament lesson. And here we are, back in our own world, standing on the threshold of another season of Advent. It begins today—that season of hopeful anticipation in which we are called to lift up our hearts and rejoice because our redemption is drawing near.

To be honest about it, I am not sure that I am ready for that event or that I can "get up" for it. Perhaps you feel the same way. After all, what reasons are there to make us feel hopeful about our world? The world is a mess, and we know it. How shall we even begin to describe it? It will be a long time before we can even say the word "Vietnam" without a shudder, remembering the horror and the futility of all that we did there in the name of peace. The all-out fighting has ceased in the Middle East, but no one believes that peace has been achieved there either. And for all of the rhetoric about détente with China and Russia, it is a fact that the great nations of the world—and some of the lesser ones too—are still striving to expand their nuclear weapon capacity, building their arsenals and developing more sophisticated delivery systems; so that the survival of the world hangs more and more on the delicate strands of the emotional stability of a few leaders. Hardly a comforting thought!

The specter of mass starvation and social chaos in the world haunts us in the night, and in our own nation, crisis has followed crisis until we are shocked into numbness. The crisis of moral leadership at the top levels of government threatens to tear this nation apart at the seams. And now there is the energy crisis, creating the growing impression that our technological development has led us into a box—a box that looks suspiciously like a coffin. Our economy is in serious trouble, millions are unemployed, and inflation continues to grow.

Hopeful? What is there to be hopeful about? Oh, we have our hopes, our small hopes. We hope that we will not be cold this winter, that inflation will not outrun our fixed incomes, that there will not be a full-blown economic depression, that we will keep our health. But the *larger hopes,* the hope that things will really be set right in the world, that justice and peace shall prevail, that love shall bloom where hate now grows and men shall brothers be, they simply are too much for us!

IV

Well, that's the problem we have with Advent, isn't it? Make no mistake about it, Advent does call us to lift up our heads and look with confident hope into the future.

I know, of course, that the part of Advent on which we tend to focus seems to take us more into the past than into the future, but this happens when we look at Advent in only one of its dimensions. The full celebration of Advent involves us in something more than a symbolic reenactment of the birth of Jesus in Bethlehem—as if that were only an event of the past!

There is a sense in which each generation stands in the same time frame with reference to that event, and a sense in which that event is always something in our present. For while that event is an event in time—a part of our history—it is also an event that continues to be a part of the Eternal Now. The birth of the Christ

Child, in its inner meaning, is the coming of God to men; and the meaning of that coming is fulfilled when we see and celebrate it as a fact of our existence, when, quite literally, Christ is born anew in us and our lives are made new!

And so Advent, in its *first dimension* as the birth of Jesus Christ, calls us to lift up our heads and rejoice in the hope that our lives can be infused with joy and peace and strength!

V

But the *second dimension* demands even more of us. How can we respond to what Jesus is talking about in our New Testament lesson—the hope of the fulfillment of *all* the promises—those radical, unbelievable promises that our full redemption is drawing near?

What all of that *means* I cannot say; nor can anyone else say, except in images and dreams. It is a dream of earth made good and fair, a vision of what life could be if it were lived totally and completely in love. It is a dream of how things could be if the life of God and the life of man were so related that each glorified the other.

This is that hope of the "Second Advent." And that hope, associated as it is in our minds with bearded men carrying placards on the streets, is perhaps more than we can manage. We are, after all, reasonable and practical people. How can we hope for something we cannot even imagine? Give us the reasons, show us the signs, and then, perhaps, we can hope that kind of hope!

In the final chapter of his book *The Hungering Dark* (New York: The Seabury Press, 1969), Frederick Buechner speaks sympathetically of our difficulties in saying yes to this hope, and suggests that "maybe" is both the most that we can manage and the most that hope can ever say. And then he adds:

"Who knows what will happen? Except that in a world without God, in a way we do know. In a world without God we know at least that the thing that will happen will be a human thing, a thing no better and no worse than the most that humanity itself can be. But in a world with God, we can never know what will happen—maybe that is the most that the second coming can mean for our time—because the thing that happens then is God's thing, and that is to say a new and unimaginable and holy thing that humanity can guess at only in its wildest dreams. In a world with God, we come together in a church to celebrate, among other things, a mystery and to learn from, among other things, our ancient and discredited dreams." (PP. 123-24)

VI

So that's what Advent calls us to do! And there can be no doubt that this is our primary role as the church in the world—to celebrate and keep alive this fantastic hope.

It is no accident that Noah's ark has always been accepted as one of the major symbols portraying the nature of the church. The ark was a comic, improbable thing—and certainly not much on which to rest ones hopes for the salvation of the world. And so also is the church—that crazy, Rube Goldberg contraption, tossed this way and that on the floods of history. There is a lot of truth in the old joke about the church and Noah's ark. If it were not for the flood outside, no one *could* endure the stench on the inside! But it may just be that the church, with its fantastic dreams and hopes for a better world, carries within itself the only hope for our drowning world!

Anyway, that's what we are here for—to celebrate that hope and keep it alive for the world. And, of course we don't know what is going to happen, just as we cannot know what form God's deliverance might take. But that's not really a matter for too much concern. "Hope," said Albert Outler, "is not the projection of our wishes onto the calendar of the future; it is rather the confidence that God is holding the future open, so that its potential for meaningful participation will remain, so that life will still be fit for living and dying, secure in God's provident presence in life and death and destiny" (*Who*

Trusts in God [New York: Oxford University Press, 1968], pp. 109-10).

So Advent invites us to send out first one dove, then another, and still another—until one day the dove returns with a sign of hope. Or is it not rather the case that such a sign has already been given—the sign of the Christ Child, who, when he was grown up, said to us, "When these things begin to happen, lift up your heads because you know that your redemption is drawing near."

Old Testament Lesson: Genesis 3:1-13 and 22-24
New Testament Lesson: Luke 2:8-16

CHRISTMASTIDE

Christmas and the Search for Home

I

Some of you will remember the song "Homeward Bound," recorded by Simon and Garfunkel a few years ago. The words and the music of this song combine superbly to express the haunting loneliness of the singer, who is on an endless journey to nowhere. All the towns look the same. Everyone he sees is a stranger. And each strange face is a reminder of those familiar faces at home—the home from which he is far removed.

One would not necessarily associate this song with Christmas. It says nothing about angels, shepherds, or the Infant Jesus—or, for that matter, about Santa Claus or falling snow. It simply expresses the deep longing of a lonely man who wants to go home and—for whatever reasons—cannot go home again. And that says something about the human situation—

something which we can all understand, and which cries out for the Word Christmas speaks to our hearts.

II

There is something about Christmas that turns us homeward—if only in our dreams—with an instinct as sure as that which guides the migratory birds in their flight. What is it? It is, in part, those memories of our childhood that recall Christmas at home as a time of wonder, warmth, and joy. Perhaps it is also our feeling that home is the place we are known, loved, and accepted. That is not always the reality, of course. Only in the idealized home—the home that really never existed—are we *always* understood and accepted for what we are, and loved with a forgiving love.

Our homes are not heaven, not even when they are Christian. The reason they are not is that they are inhabited by real people—by sinners who are not yet fully redeemed. People who live in homes often hurt the others who live there— and are hurt by them. Nevertheless, our homes *are* in some degree a foretaste of the kingdom of heaven. For here (if not constantly, at least occasionally), we do experience a love that understands, forgives, and accepts.

But, is that all of it? Does that really explain

what it is that turns us towards home at Christmas? If it is in part these things I have mentioned, is there not something else at work here, something less obvious? I believe that there is; and while I cannot hope to explain it, perhaps I can point towards it.

Christmas, as the celebration of the birth of Jesus Christ, calls us to *our true home*—that home of which our earthly homes are at best only token symbols. Since this is so, the movement towards home at Christmastime may be an unconscious expression of our search for our real home—for the God in whom we live and move and have our being!

III

There are many ways in which one might describe the spirit of our times, but any true characterization would have to include the *feeling of homelessness* that is so widespread.

The social upheavals of recent decades have created millions of refugees—people who literally have no home and no homeland to which they can return. But there are millions more who are symbolically homeless. The places and structures where their hearts and their hopes once rested either no longer exist or are changed beyond recognition or acceptance. Their churches, their political parties, their communities are not what they used to be—or what, at least, they were perceived to be. They feel that everything has changed or is changing. They feel alienated from all that once established their identity.

Someone was talking to me just recently about one of our church members who feels alienated in this way. "Is there something which I have done to hurt his feelings towards the church?" I asked. "No," came the reply, "it has nothing to do with you, except insofar as you may be a symbol of change. He simply feels that his church and the Democratic party have gone off and left him." I understand that feeling. And there isn't much anyone can do about it—except understand it.

But deeper still—and even more disturbing—is the feeling of not being as close to God as we once were. I find that this feeling is widespread among us, and that it appears in all age groups. Why this should be so is something we could talk about at some length; but it is enough to say now that this *is* the climate of our times. It appears to be a fact that ours is not an "age of faith."

I recently saw on television a production of Thornton Wilder's play *Our Town*, which has its setting in the years just before World War I. As I watched the play unfold, I was struck anew with the tremendous changes that have occurred in our general outlook on life, especially in regard to our feeling of being at home in a secure faith in God.

There is a scene in this play in which one of the young people is telling another about a letter one of her friends has received from her minister.

"He wrote Jane a letter and on the envelope the address was like this: It said: Jane Crofut; The Crofut Farm; Grovers Corners; Sutton County; New Hampshire; United States of America."

"What's funny about that?"

"But listen, it's not finished: The United States of America; Continent of North America; Western Hemisphere; the Earth; the Solar System; the Universe; the Mind of God—that's what it said on the envelope. . . . And the postman brought it just the same."

How remote and nostalgic all of that appears in our times—especially that secure feeling of being at home in the mind of God! And perhaps the Christmas story itself appears just as remote from our real world—and as unrecoverable as some long-lost experience of our naïve childhood. But we can at least look at and listen to it (and not without hope); for it is not merely something back there in the distant past. It is God calling us to come to our true home, and it is God opening the door for us!

IV

The Christmas story has a history, of course. It did not just happen like a bolt out of the blue. Its background goes all the way back to our Old Testament lesson. That story in Genesis 3 speaks to our sense of alienation, to our feeling of being "outside of Paradise." And the whole story of the Old Testament is a kind of history of man's journey towards his true home, led on by God.

If you want a beginning point, then say that it began with Abraham, who left his prosperous home and became a wanderer in response to God's call. Abraham became an enduring symbol of faith; and the word that characterized this period of man's spiritual history was "Go!" "Go out!" "Now the Lord said to Abram, 'Go from your country and your kindred and your father's house to the land that I will show you'" (Gen. 12:1).

From then on the people of faith were wanderers in search of a home—right on down to the time of Mary and Joseph, who in obedience to God's call went out from their home to go up to Bethlehem. And suddenly—right there— everything undergoes a radical change!

If the Christmas story really *begins* with Abraham, as the wanderer in search of a home, it *ends* with everyone running towards

Bethlehem—and with the feeling that now at last they have come home! The angels' announcement to the shepherds: "To you is born this day in the city of David a Savior, who is Christ the Lord" (Luke 2:11), sets everything in motion. But now it is not an aimless wandering; it is motion directed to one spot and one person: "And they went with haste, and found Mary and Joseph, and the babe lying in a manger" (Luke 2:16).

From here on in the New Testament the word spoken to the people of faith is "Come." *Come* to Bethlehem and see him whose birth the angels sing. It is Christ himself standing among men and saying: "Come to me, all who labor and are heavy laden, and I will give you rest" (Matt. 11:28). Here then at last—here and nowhere else upon the earth—is our true home. And we are lonely wanderers upon the earth until we have found it!

V

Bethlehem is our true home. But what does it mean to say that? It is a poetic way of saying that here is the place—the event—where there appears in its fullness that love that is only partially and occasionally glimpsed in our earthly homes. Here is that Divine Love that is steadfast and unlimited and from which no one is excluded. Here is that love in which we are fully known and fully accepted and in which we find our real identity.

Therefore, Christmas brings before us something that is both *a reality* and *a hope*. It is a reality in that this love of God has appeared as related by the Christmas story. And it is a hope in that men have not everywhere—and nowhere completely—recognized, received, and reflected that love. If they had done so, then no one would be hungry and homeless and lonely in our midst; nor would bitterness and strife exist between races and nations, because men would everywhere accept one another as brothers within their Father's house. And that, we sadly confess, is not how things are in this world. Still, that is the hope the Christmas story unfolds. Its message of Peace hangs over our violent world as the Christmas star hangs over the manger in Bethlehem, and it is the only hope that lightens our darkening way.

Homeward bound? Yes—we hope so. And now at last we know at least where home is!

VI

What I have wanted to say in this sermon can be fully expressed only in poetry. So I will let the poets speak last.

Charles Williams paints the Nativity scene in

words, and includes in his painting—in addition to the shepherds, the wise men, and the beasts—none other than Adam, the same Adam who was turned out of Paradise. And he has Joseph saying: "Father Adam, come in, here is your child, here is the Son of Man, here is Paradise. Today everything begins again."

G. K. Chesterton wrote a poem about Bethlehem that says it all:

> To an open house in the evening,
> Home shall men come,
> To an older place than Eden,
> And a taller town than Rome.
> To the end of the way of the wandering star,
> To the things that cannot be and that are,
> To the place where God was homeless,
> And all men are at home.
>   "The House of Christmas"

EPIPHANY

Revelation and Mystery

I

That a bush should be on fire in the desert was not strange; but that it should burn and burn and not be consumed, that was very strange indeed! So Moses turned aside to contemplate this mystery. When he did so, the mystery deepened. He was sure that God was speaking to him—and surely God is the ultimate mystery!

This story contains that fascinating combination of *revelation* and *mystery* that appears throughout the Scriptures. Note here that the one who speaks to Moses remains hidden. He tells Moses something of his purpose, and he assigns to Moses a specific task; but he himself remains hidden and mysterious. He identifies himself as "the God of your forefathers, the God of Abraham, Isaac, and Jacob," but more than that he will not disclose. When Moses presses God for his name (i.e., a more precise definition of

33

himself), God replies: "I am; that is who I am," or, as the phrase may also be translated, "I will be what I will be" (Exod. 3:14 NEB).

II

This story may serve first to remind us of something that has been all but lost from our lives—*our sensitivity to the mystery that lies all around us*. Moses could see the burning bush in the desert and respond to it in terms of what it was—a mystery. He could do this because he was sensitive to the presence of mystery all around him. But it is not so with us. We live in a world that is intolerant of mystery, and that tends to equate mystery with the unreal.

A story is told of a little boy whose father expressed the usual before-dinner command: "Hurry up and wash your hands and come to prayers." As the boy went towards the bathroom, he was heard to mutter: "Germs and Jesus, germs and Jesus! That's all I hear around here, and I can't see either one of them!" That is both a funny and a sad story. It suggests how our unspoken assumptions are communicated so accurately to our children. And in this case the unspoken assumption is that if you can't see it, feel it, taste it, hear it, or smell it, it isn't real!

Man in the scientific age has been obsessed with the idea of knowing and explaining everything. Everything must be understood, cataloged, and placed within an ordered scheme of things. No loose ends! And no place for mystery! With our scientific methods we have probed and penetrated the mysteries of both man and nature. We have observed, analyzed, and organized the data, and run it through our computers—until it seems that whatever has escaped us could hardly be significant and probably not real. Freud is reported to have said, "If Science cannot discover it, it just isn't there." That expressed what has been for some time now the climate of the modern world.

It is not surprising, then, that our confidence in the validity of that dimension of life that *cannot* be measured or tested by the scientific method has been undermined. The seriousness of this as it affects the climate for faith is quite obvious. If we have eliminated mystery from the scene, we have eliminated God and all possibility of knowing and believing in God. And bringing in "revelation" will not alter that fact, because what is revealed is also a mystery. For whatever else God may be, he is and will always continue to be a mystery—the mystery—the haunting, ineffable mystery of our existence.

III

Something is happening today, something that is not necessarily what one would have expected a few years ago. Something is happening that suggests people in the modern world are hungry for mystery and hence are potential believers in God—perhaps even in the God who reveals the mystery of his presence in the ways related in the Scriptures. There are all manner of signs around that suggest human beings are simply not able to endure a life that has been stripped of mystery. We do, and must, reach out for something beyond ourselves that will invest life with some transcendent meaning, something beyond eating and sleeping, working and spending, suffering and dying.

Perhaps this explains why religion persists, and why it will always be a part of the human experience in one form or another. "The word *religion* points to that area of human experience where one way or another man comes upon Mystery as a summons to pilgrimage; where he senses beyond and beneath the realities of every day a Reality no less real because it can only be hinted at in myths and rituals; where he glimpses a destination that he can never fully know until he reaches it" (Frederick Buechner, *Wishful Thinking* [New York: Harper & Row, 1973], p.

78). As Paul Lehmann recently preached: "The testimony of the human story overwhelmingly points to the formative power of mystery over matter-of-factness in the experience of being human in the world. Indeed, religion is so basic to and ineradicable from the human condition because religion is the persistent pursuit of the formative power of mystery over matter-of-factness in human affairs."

So it would appear that man remains an incurable believer, even in the scientific age. He does not really change his character as a believer; he only changes the character of his beliefs. Believing in something beyond himself seems to be intrinsic to his nature. He simply cannot live the life from which the mystery has been extracted.

IV

What this new appreciation of the dimension of mystery in human life says about the viability of Christian faith remains to be seen. But it does at least open up possibilities for faith in the God who reveals himself as the God and Father of our Lord Jesus Christ. And there is some ground for hope that it may lead to a rediscovery of the Scriptures, the knowledge of which has been lost almost completely from our common cultural life.

I say this about the Scriptures because they, if nothing else, do at least provide us with a language for thinking and talking about the mystery of God. We need such a language, and modern culture does not provide us with one. The language of the Scriptures is still viable, therefore. It is full of images, symbols, and metaphors that enable us to talk about both "the presence of mystery" and "the mystery of presence"—at least they do if we don't insist upon imposing on them our literal-mindedness. And that may be a problem for some of us.

We preachers of the Word have not always been as open as we might have been in helping our hearers understand some things about the basic character of the Scriptures. We have been afraid to use the words "myth" and "symbol." But there is no way we can have religion without mystery, and there is no way we can talk about the ultimate without using the language of myth and symbols—those speech forms that point beyond themselves to the mystery they can never capture in *any* words.

As an example of what I mean here, consider the first three chapters of Genesis. These stories of the creation and the fall of man should be understood as "myth." It will avoid a lot of confusion if we say clearly that this is *how* we understand them. To say that they are myth, however, is not to say that they are untrue. It is simply to say that they were never intended to be understood as scientific or historical accounts but that they do express something about God and man that we want to affirm as being always and everywhere true. Myth, in this sense, is a word for that "picture language" we must use to speak of those realities that cannot be captured by scientific and historical examination. So let these stories in Genesis stand as they are, enshrining the mystery and majesty of God and the mystery and majesty of man created by God. They point beyond themselves to that which cannot be fully expressed in our language, always saying more than we can say about them.

V

But some of you will surely be thinking something like this: "Yes, but we Christians believe that God has now revealed himself in his Living Word, Jesus Christ. And does not this mean that we have now moved beyond myth and mystery? Does not this mean that now the mystery has been stripped away, so that we have seen 'the glory of God in the face of Christ'?"

Let me answer those questions with some other questions. Is God's revelation of himself in Jesus Christ so clear and unambiguous as to remove the necessity for faith and personal commitment? Is it not rather the case that Jesus Christ himself is the greatest mystery ever to confront us? What else can you make of these words from the prologue of the Gospel according to John: "In the beginning was the Word, and the Word was with God, and the Word was God. . . . And the Word became flesh and dwelt among us"?

At Caesarea Phillipi, Jesus raised the question of his identity with his disciples—the inner circle. First he asked how others were answering that question. They answered, giving some of the current opinions and speculations. So then he asked, "But who do *you* say that I am?" And Simon Peter answered, "You are the Christ, the Son of the living God." Jesus accepted that as a true insight, but he recognized and underscored the fact that this was *a faith perception*, not a rational conclusion drawn inevitably from the observable facts. He said: "Blessed are you, Simon Bar-Jona! For flesh and blood has not revealed this to you, but my Father who is in heaven."

What we are witnessing here in this scene is that revelation which is "the revelation of mystery." God is a mystery—the ultimate mystery! Even in his revelation, God continues to be the Lord, the one whose thoughts are not our thoughts and whose ways are not our ways. He appears as one who is unconditionally *for* us, but never as one who is available to our control or manipulation. He will not appear as the undeniable, self-evident fact, to be used as the linchpin for a system of thought or the justification of any society's way of life! Always he appears in that hiddenness and mystery that is a part of his nature—open to those who want to know him in order to serve him and closed to those who want only to know about him or to use him for their own purposes.

When the church speaks of God's "revelation," then, it is not saying that now the mystery has been stripped away from God. It is saying, rather, that in Jesus Christ God gives us *a sign of his presence*, and that for those who will turn aside and look at this sign, God speaks and discloses something of himself we would otherwise never experience.

VI

What confronts us most centrally in the Christian faith is the person of Jesus Christ. And let it be said most emphatically that he himself is a mystery! The New Testament equivalent for the burning bush in the Old Testament is Jesus Christ. And Jesus Christ is a mystery and a source of wonder, a light that shines on in our darkness, a burning bush that is not consumed, a sign through which the Eternal Mystery speaks to faith!

That sign is with us, just as it has been with other generations before us. It calls us to turn aside, to look and to listen, to ponder and to wonder. Given that willingness on our part, faith is a possibility for us, just as much as it was for Moses and for Peter.

LENT

Examining Our Desires

I

"Ho, every one who thirsts, come to the waters; and he who has no money, come, buy and eat!" (Isa. 55:1). "Ask, and it will be given you; seek, and you will find; knock, and it will be opened to you. For every one who asks receives, and he who seeks finds, and to him who knocks it will be opened" (Matt. 7:7-8).

What comes to your mind when you hear these words from the Scriptures? Perhaps there is something about them that disturbs you, even as it disturbs me. God appears so willing to give us what we ask. His resources are so graciously placed within our reach. And somehow this leaves us with a nagging question that begins to worm its way to the surface of our minds. *Why, if this is so, are we not more than we are as persons and as Christians?*

43

All of us have some kind of image of what a Christian ought to be, but few of us would say that this image fits us. So what is the problem? Is there no balm in Gilead that we are not healed? Or is there perhaps some other reason? This story from John 5 may throw some light on these questions.

The pool of Bethesda in Jerusalem was a gathering place for invalids from all over the country. Legend held that from time to time an angel stirred the waters and that when this happened, whoever stepped into the waters first would be healed. We may properly regard that as mere superstition, but the people of that time believed it; and that is why the sick, the lame, and the blind gathered there. On one particular visit to Jerusalem Jesus went immediately to this place. Looking over the pathetic scene, he singled out one man, walked over to him, and asked this question: "Do you want to be healed?"

In the context of this scene, this question has the grace of the proverbial elephant in the china closet! It seems, at the least, unnecessary—and even heartless—not at all in keeping with that sensitivity and gentleness usually shown by Jesus in his dealings with people. Wasn't it obvious that this man wanted to be healed? Why else would he be there? Why then must Jesus ask this heartless question? The answer is that Jesus was too realistic to assume that our desires are what they appear to be on the surface. That is why he addressed this question to the lame man, and it was necessary that he do so.

After all, this man had been paralysed for thirty-eight years. Thirty-eight long years! And most of that time had been spent there beside this pool, just waiting. Perhaps something has happened to him during those years, something that he himself has failed to recognize. His condition had demanded an adjustment that had not been easy to make; but once made, and long accepted, would it not then be extremely difficult to readjust his life to the demands and responsibilities of health and wholeness?

Look at it this way. Life at Bethesda had its compensations. It was not altogether unpleasant to lie there in the cool porches while well men were toiling outside under the blazing sun. Everyone who looked at him could see that he was helpless; so no one expected anything from him. Some kind persons must have fed and clothed him. The fare may not have been the best, but he had grown accustomed to it. No doubt health was a good thing, but this way of life, once grown accustomed to, had its own compensations.

And so, you see, *Jesus had to ask this question*. Did this man really *want* to be healed, knowing what it would cost him in terms of a radical change in his life-style? It was something that had to be considered. And Jesus had to know, because God himself cannot give us health and wholeness unless that is what we really want. Now, as it turned out, this man *did* want to be healed; and he *was* healed!

II

"Do you want to be healed?" I wonder if we have the courage to let Jesus address that question to us! I wonder because we can see already that this question is going to work us into a corner. But never mind that; let's face it anyway. Actually, we are not left with any choice about that. If we want to hear this story as the Word of God for us, then we must identify with this lame man. And, having substituted our spiritual infirmity for his physical infirmity, we must face the searching implications of that question, Do you want to be healed? Do we really want what Jesus is ready to give us, and what we say we want, or are we simply deceiving ourselves about our real desires?

Now we begin to see what it is that disturbs us whenever we hear these generous offers from God! Aware of our spiritual poverty, we are forced to conclude either that God is simply putting us on or that we really don't want what he offers. What other conclusion *could* we reach? "If you will stop and ask yourself why you are not as pious as the primitive Christians," said William Law, "your own heart will tell you that it is neither through ignorance nor inability, but purely because you never thoroughly intended it."

Kipling liked to say that if we have not gotten from life what we wanted, this is proof that we did not really want it—or else we tried to haggle about the price. I cannot swallow that bit of philosophy entirely. All of us have some limiting factors in our lives that cannot be changed by any intensity of desire. But we can take Kipling's statement and apply it unreservedly to what *God* offers us. I repeat—to what God offers us—not just to anything that we might happen to want.

Let's be sure that we are clear on what it is that God does offer us. He does not offer us houses and lands; nor does he promise that if we will only follow his Son we will enjoy good health, be free from the burden of suffering, and have a long and happy life. God does not always give us what we ask for, no matter how intensely we might desire it. From the early years of my ministry, I remember a young woman who had cancer. In spite of good medical treatment and her own faith and prayers, she grew steadily worse. One day when I visited her, she told me of a dream she had had the night before. She dreamed that an angel had come from God and touched her and that the mass in her abdomen had dissolved. No doubt this dream was an expression of her real and intense desire to be healed. But she was not healed, and shortly thereafter she died.

At this point I want to express my reservations concerning the so-called faith healers who are so numerous in our culture today. Perhaps a few persons are healed of their physical infirmities through their ministrations, but what about the harm done to so many others who are told that if they only had faith they could be healed? God is misrepresented in all of this. Jesus indeed healed a few persons of their physical ills. Note that he healed one—and only one—among that crowd by the pool of Bethesda. Why him and not any of the others? Why did he do it at all? I do not know all the answers to those questions, but John suggests that these rare instances of healing were signs to point us to a deeper kind of healing. And certainly Jesus never made any wholesale promise of the healing of our physical infirmities.

What God *does* offer us is something else. He offers us sufficient resources for the handling of these problems. He offers us the riches that money cannot buy—truth, integrity, a sense of purpose, the fellowship of Jesus Christ and the apostles, and a certain peace and joy that nothing can take from us. All of this God offers us, without reservations. So if we do not have these things, then it is hard for us to deny Kipling's thesis—either we do not want them or else we have tried to haggle the price!

III

The price? But where does that come into the picture? Doesn't Isaiah have God saying, "Come, buy wine and milk *without* money and *without* price"? and doesn't Jesus himself say, "Ask, and it will be *given?*" (italics added). How then do we end up here talking about the price?

The reality that confronts us here is paradoxical, but it is not foreign to our own experience of life. Life always confronts us with a multiplicity of choices. There are many ways we might go, and the choice of one way excludes the possibility of another. Thus, the price we pay for going one way is the possible gain from having gone one of the other ways—a truth immortalized by Robert Frost in his poem "The Road Not Taken."

So, what God offers us is that which we could neither earn nor buy; nevertheless, it has a kind of price tag on it. We have to want it enough to seek it, to seek it more than we seek something else. We can't have everything, you know! There isn't that much time. There isn't that much of us to spend. And it really doesn't mean anything at all for me to say that I want something unless I can say what I want it *more than!*

Don't ever treat this little word "ask" as if it were the simplest word in the world. It isn't, and neither are these words "seek" and "knock." All three of these are *active verbs,* suggesting in the context of our New Testament lesson an action that is urgent, insistent, and prompted by an intense desire.

IV

What is pressing us here is the necessity of examining our desires with an unflinching honesty. And that would be a proper undertaking for us in this Lenten season. Lent calls us to repent because the kingdom of heaven is at hand. The process of repentance must begin with an honest examination of our real desires. What do we really want in life? Do we want what God offers us in Jesus Christ?

Let us be very careful how we answer that question. Self-deception comes very easily here. One of our usual answers is: "Yes, of course, but *not now.* Later on I really do intend to get with it—but not right now." Another of our answers, equally unacceptable, is: "Yes, of course I want what God offers—but *not all* of it." But we can't get God to play that game, and we know it. The trouble with that, suggested C. S. Lewis, is that it is like going to the dentist with a toothache. You really do want to get that tooth fixed, but once the dentist gets to poking around in there, he sees all manner of problems and starts talking about fixing teeth that haven't even started to ache yet!

"Do you want to be made whole?" Jesus asked the man at Bethesda. Note that he did not ask: "Would you like a bandaid? A shot to ease your pain? Could I get you a new bed or a better set of crutches?" No, Jesus asked, "Do you want to be made whole?" He was asking this man if he wanted a total cure—something that would change his whole way of life!

How would *we* have answered if we had been that man? If? Why say "if"? I really wonder if that whole scene at Bethesda is not an accurate symbolic representation of who we are and where we are today as the church! A bunch of cripples—the lame, the blind, the paralyzed—all gathered at what is reputed to be a place of healing. Supposedly we are here because we want to be healed, but the years go by and go by and we are not healed. Actually, we rather like it here, and if we know and admit that we are not yet whole—well, it is at least comforting to know that God forgives us.

But what if Christ really is here with the power of God to heal us! What if he is able to say, "Get up and walk!"—and willing to say it, too, if what we really want is healing and wholeness, not sedatives or better crutches.

When *will* we be really alive and free? When will we be mature and responsible Christians? When will the church be able to rise up and walk, ready to move on out in mission? The answer to that is simply this—when that is what we want—really want! God's power *is* present in Jesus Christ to heal us, to enable us to grow up into the stature of Christ. But God will not say, "Get up and walk" until that is what we really want!

EASTERTIDE

The Resurrection of Jesus Christ—
Spiritual Symbol or Historical Reality?

I

"Why is the preacher speaking on that subject at this time?" That question is usually present in the mind of any thoughtful listener in the pew, and I suspect that it came to your mind as soon as you noted the printed title of this sermon. Perhaps your thoughts were something like this: "Easter Sunday is already behind us. He certainly knows that! So why has he chosen to preach about the resurrection today?"

There are two reasons for my decision, and I will share them with you. First, I am convinced that if we talk about the resurrection only at Easter, it tends to get isolated, and we are encouraged to think of the resurrection as a thing in itself, apart from the rest of the Gospel story. This, in turn, leads to the assumption that we can treat the resurrection as *an optional feature* of the Christian faith. Second, I am convinced that the resurrection is, for many Christians, more a source of *embarrassment* than a source of *assurance*. While we would not go so far as to put it in the category of a ghost story, it does seem to border on the superstitious. It is not uncommon to encounter the assumption that to affirm the resurrection is somehow "less intelligent" than to question or deny it. Some of us may have fallen for that assumption.

That both of these notions—that the resurrection of Jesus Christ is an optional feature of faith and that an affirmation of the resurrection is a sign of lesser intelligence—are false is something I hope to demonstrate in this sermon. So, let's start with them.

II

What the New Testament proclaims, basically, can be expressed in three words, and those words are: *Christ is risen!* It is obvious, of course, that the New Testament has other things to say and that it uses many more words in which to say them. Nevertheless, it must be stated as a fact that every word in the New Testament was written from the perspective of "Christ is risen" and that, as Paul demonstrates for the Corinthians, if you abstract those words, the whole story falls apart! "The gospel," says Richard Niebuhr, "cannot be abstracted from the proclamation that Christ *is* risen."

In speaking of those who want to believe in Jesus but not in his resurrection from the dead, James D. Smart says: "They need to make clear to themselves what place a Jesus who did not rise from the dead has in a creed that is essentially . . . and certainly in all it says of Jesus, a confession of faith in God. The resurrection does not and cannot stand alone. Its removal makes necessary the writing of another creed that will speak differently in *all* of its articles" (*The Creed in Christian Teaching* [Philadelphia: The Westminster Press, 1962], p. 56).

Now, there have been very few scholars desiring to take a position other than that, but the question still remains, What do the writers *mean* when they say Christ is risen? Do they intend us to understand that they are using the language of myth and symbol? Or do they mean us to understand that they are talking about an event—about something that actually happened?

Since the dawn of the modern age, in which men have been more or less inclined to exclude from reality that which they cannot verify scientifically, there have been many prominent New Testament scholars who have attempted to "spiritualize" the resurrection in one way or another. This effort has taken a variety of forms, but basically they all say the same thing: the resurrection of Jesus was in reality the resurrection of faith in the hearts and minds of the disciples. The suggestion is offered that some time after Jesus' death the disciples found that Jesus seemed still to be with them in a spiritual sense, and so they chose to describe this experience in stories cast in the framework of "historical event." The stories, however, were not intended to be taken literally.

Now that sounds reasonable at first, but whatever plausability it has seems to disappear when we examine the way the writers actually speak of the resurrection. Clearly, it is the language of event. They are talking about a resurrected Jesus who came to them *unexpectedly*, one who could be seen, heard, and touched. Further, the story includes the tradition of the empty tomb, a tradition that was included and accepted by the early church deliberately, and that cannot on any logical basis be eliminated.

In our New Testament lesson I Corinthians 15, Paul speaks in one and the same sentence about Jesus' crucifixion, death, burial, *and* resurrection from the dead on the third day. I fail to see the logic in suggesting that three of these are actual, historical events, while the fourth is only a spiritual truth expressed in that form.

I suggest, then, that what the witnesses meant

by "Christ is risen" is fairly clear. Whether they
were right or wrong in their perception is
another question. Whether or not we believe
them is also another question. On these matters
we are free; but are not free to rewrite the New
Testament.

III

I have already suggested that the resurrection
of Jesus, as related in the New Testament, is not
an optional feature of the Christian faith. To
justify that statement we have only to remind
ourselves what is at stake here, namely, the
identity of Jesus and the character of God.

> Jesus Christ, Jesus Christ,
> Who are you? What have you sacrificed?

Those plaintive words from *Jesus Christ
Superstar* raise the crucial question that is
answered only by the resurrection—or by its
absence! If it all ended abruptly at the cross, why
then Jesus was just another Jewish rabbi; and
while his teachings have an enduring charm, he
was actually mistaken in most of his basic
assumptions, and especially in what he taught
about God.

What is at stake here is the nature of God and
whether or not God is free to act or has acted in

history to confront and overcome the powers of sin and death. For if when the best in man meets the worst in man God stands by letting the conflict run its course, then we are right back where we started. The history of Jesus? It was just one more chapter in an old, old story—the victory of the powers of darkness and death over goodness, justice, and love!

But that, most decidedly, is *not* the way the New Testament tells the story! In the words of Peter, speaking on the day of Pentecost: "Let all the house of Israel therefore know assuredly that God has made him both Lord and Christ, this Jesus whom you crucified" (Acts 2:36).

IV

Let us look now at that other false assumption I said I wanted to explore, the assumption that since there really is no hard evidence to support the New Testament claim that Jesus was raised from the dead, the resurrection can be affirmed only at the sacrifice of our highest intelligence.

In speaking to this point, Markus Barth once said: "The arguments proffered to disprove the historicity of the resurrection are at least as dogmatically prejudiced and fallible as the arguments to the contrary." I most certainly agree with that statement! Further, I make bold to suggest that there *is* a considerable body of evidence to support the claim of the primitive church that Christ *is* risen.

Such evidence is not, of course, scientific proof; nor should we expect it to be such. God simply does not deal with us on that level. He never attempts to offer us objective, infallible proof of his reality. If he should do so, there would be no room for either our freedom or our faith. His restraint is intentional. Nevertheless, there are signs which *do* support faith. There *is* evidence to support the resurrection claim—at least enough to suggest that those who affirm it are not necessarily more naïve or less intelligent than others.

The point is that something happened back there—something that had discernible consequences. And however we decide to explain it, the explanation ought to be big enough to fit the facts! Here are two facts that would seem to be beyond dispute:

First, the disciples were turned around— suddenly, dramatically, radically. If we can at all trust the honesty of the record, all of the disciples forsook him and fled as he died upon the cross. They were hiding out in the attics of Jerusalem, in fear of the authorities. Further, it seems clear that they were in despair—and why not? The dream in which they had invested so much was now hopelessly shattered. But suddenly the picture changes, and we see these same men filled with a radiant faith, speaking courageously and acting boldly!

Second, a community was created. Suddenly we are confronted with a group of remarkably joyful, courageous, and dedicated people who in the space of a few years have set the world talking about Jesus Christ and launched a faith and a community that has worked a change in the life of the world to a remarkable degree, one that has not yet by any means been played out after two thousand years!

Anyone here who would like to try doing that? Anyone here who would like to have a go at writing something comparable to the New Testament? Obviously, then, something happened—something that requires some explanation big enough to fit the facts. Their explanation was offered in those crucial three words: *He is risen!*

Other explanations might be offered—and have been—but I can only say that I do not find any of them very convincing.

But let me say again that this is only evidence—evidence that will carry whatever weight we assign to it. It is not infallible proof, and is not offered as such. Faith in the resurrection is still just that—faith.

V

Since this is so, we find ourselves in the position in which potential disciples have always found themselves—listening to the witnesses and having to decide whether or not we can say amen to what they affirm.

God approaches us as he has always approached men—in a hidden kind of disclosure—in such a way that only in faith can we discern and decide.

Therefore, the proclamation "He is Risen" calls for our discernment and our decision. Here we are, faced with the proclamation of an astounding event that, if true, changes the whole meaning of our human existence. We cannot change that proclamation, just as most of us cannot dismiss it casually. We cannot prove that it is true, just as we cannot prove that it is not true. The discussions could go on endlessly, but life does not stand still while we try to settle matters by our discussions. The crucial matters must always be settled by decisions and actions or else we lose the options by default.

Has Christ been raised from the dead and declared by God to be the lord of men and nations? *Has* God vindicated the words and the faith of Jesus by this mighty act? Is this really God's world, so that I can put my trust in his goodness and love for this life and in my death?

Let me be the first to admit that it is not easy to do that—or even for me to claim that in fact I do it! I must confess that there are times, at least, when my faith is hard-pressed by doubts. And all the while, life itself is pressing me for a decision—a decision that cannot be made by words alone. Therefore I must accept the fact that the statement "I believe while I doubt, and I doubt while I believe" is both an honest confession and an acceptable faith. And, probably, it is the only kind of faith possible for sinful men. But perhaps I should say that it is the only kind of faith I have attained.

All of us might wish for a stronger kind of faith, but there is a sense in which that really is not too important. What really matters is this: To which side of the question are we drawn? Given a choice, where do we take our stand? Am I willing to live my life by faith in the resurrection or not? That is the issue, and to state it any other way is an evasion.

We *do* have a choice! In the midst of life's uncertainties we can choose that faith on which we shall build our lives—and act accordingly. The gospel asks nothing more than that, and nothing less!

EASTERTIDE

Faith Is a Gift

I

That the story of the Emmaus Road is a story of singular grace and haunting beauty is evident to all who have ever read it or heard it. What is *not* necessarily evident is that this is a highly sophisticated story, carefully shaped by Luke to serve a specific purpose.

In saying that Luke "shaped" the story, I am not suggesting that he made it up. There is no reason to doubt that two disciples had experienced something that was essentially as the story related it. Luke knew the story well because it circulated widely in the early church and was a part of the whole resurrection tradition. What I am suggesting is that Luke took the story, shaped it in its present form, and used it for his own purpose. His purpose was very theological. He wanted to speak to those in the church who were troubled with radical doubt about the

63

resurrection of Jesus. What we have here, then, is theology in the form of a story—a carefully constructed story, suggests Hans Dieter Betz. In an article for *Interpretation* (January 1969), he wrote: "Certainly, nothing told in the narrative is incidental; every detail has its significance. It is the intention of this legend to tell what is essential to the origin and nature of the Christian faith."

I am suggesting that if we approach the story from this perspective, it will open itself to us with a new and richer meaning.

II

It may come as a surprise to us to learn that some of those who were closest to Jesus were troubled with radical doubts. We know about our own struggle for faith, and looking at those first disciples through rose-colored glasses, we envy them for their stalwart, unwavering faith. We see them as simple persons for whom faith came easy. Or perhaps we imagine them to have had supporting evidence that is not available to us.

Indeed, we seem to think that serious doubt about extraordinary occurrences is a phenomenon of the modern mind, stemming from the scientific world view. Therefore, we tend to see belief and doubt in the New Testament in terms of black and white. We recognize, of course, that some people did not believe in the resurrection, but those who did, did so with an unshaken assurance. Or so we think! It is hard for us to visualize a skeptical frame of mind among the apostles, or to understand that they had to wrestle with radical doubt within themselves and among their converts.

But in fact they did struggle with doubt. A careful reading of the New Testament reveals that many of the writers recognized this problem and spoke to it. For instance, in the closing verses of his Gospel, Matthew recognizes that such doubts existed even within the ranks of the first eleven disciples: "Now the eleven disciples went to Galilee, to the mountain to which Jesus had directed them. And when they saw him they worshiped him; *but some doubted*" (Matt. 28:16-17 [italics added]). And there is *Paul* writing his monumental chapter on the resurrection, saying to the church in Corinth, "How can some of you say that there is no resurrection of the dead?" (I Cor. 15:12*b*). Obviously, Paul would not have written that if he had not been aware of the radical doubts that existed among some of that congregation.

And that is the problem to which Luke is speaking in the Emmaus story. If you want a "theological outline" of it—and I think that Luke

himself had one in mind—it would go something
like this:

A. Recognition of the cruciality of the resurrection for Christian faith.
B. Recognition of the ambiguity of the evidence for the resurrection.
C. Recognition of the origin and nature of faith
in the risen Christ.

III

A. THE CRUCIALITY OF THE
RESURRECTION FOR CHRISTIAN FAITH

In our story, two sad disciples are trudging
along the road from Jerusalem to Emmaus. They
are overtaken by a stranger. We know who he is,
but they do not, even though they had been
eyewitnesses of recent events in Jerusalem. The
stranger overhears their conversation and in-
quires what they are talking about. Since he also
appears to be coming from Jerusalem, they are
surprised that he should ask. "Are you the only
visitor to Jerusalem who does not know the
things that have happened there in these days?"
"What things?" he replies, and they answer:
"Concerning Jesus of Nazareth, who was a
prophet mighty in deed and word before God and
all the people, and how our chief priests and
rulers delivered him up to be condemned to

death, and crucified him. *But we had hoped that he was the one to redeem Israel"* (italics added).

We had hoped! No wonder these disciples were sad and weary! They were carrying the burden of a dead hope—the heaviest of all burdens! *We had hoped—but now it is all over and we are going home.*

That's what the story of Jesus comes down to, isn't it, if there is no resurrection? Men are not inspired by a dead hope. They may for a while gather around a lost cause to mourn it, to keep its memory alive; but the lost cause does not survive for long, nor does it set men on their feet and send them running through the world shouting, "Good news!"

It is no exaggeration to say that we would not be here today, that there would be no church and no New Testament from which to read such stories, if there had not been disciples who were convinced that Jesus had been raised from the dead and thus was still alive and present with them. J. Moltmann states the issue precisely when he says: "Christianity stands or falls with the reality of the raising of Jesus from the dead by God. In the New Testament there is no faith that does not start a priori with the resurrection of Jesus."

Paul stated the matter quite bluntly for the Corinthians many years before: "If Christ has not been raised, then our preaching is in vain and your faith is in vain." Preaching? What is there to preach? Faith? What is there to believe in, if the story grinds to a halt in the tomb? The hope that God cares about what happens on earth, the hope that love is stronger than sin and death, the hope that Jesus was sent by the Father—all of these hopes are buried and sealed in Christ's tomb if that is where the story ends!

What Paul states propositionally, Luke states pictorially in his story of two disciples walking a weary road with the burden of a dead hope. It is as if Luke were saying to his readers: "Look, I understand the problem you have with the resurrection; but you may as well face the facts honestly. If there is no resurrection, there is no gospel. You have nothing left but a dead hope."

B. THE AMBIGUITY OF THE EVIDENCE FOR THE RESURRECTION

Well, does it really help to be told that? Perhaps it does not. It may make us even more uneasy. What if I cannot believe? I fear that this does not help if that is all that Luke can say. But of course that isn't all—only we must be a bit patient. What he says next may make the problem even worse for some! For he has these two disciples saying: "Some women of our company amazed us. They were at the tomb early in the morning and did not find his body; and they came back saying that they had even seen a vision of angels, who said that he was alive. Some of those who were with us went to the tomb, and found it just as the women had said; but him they did not see."

I think that in these verses Luke is recognizing quite honestly the ambiguity of the evidence for the resurrection. Here we have a story of an empty tomb and a vision of angels, told by some disciples who may have been hysterical with grief. Is that evidence? Well, it is evidence of a kind; but it is far less than conclusive proof, and obviously it had not been convincing for these two disciples who were relating it.

And the fact is that *all* accounts of the resurrection in the New Testament incorporate this ambiguity. There is no witness who claims to have seen the resurrection actually taking place. The tomb was empty; that seems to be a hard fact one need hardly question. But does that necessarily indicate a resurrection? Other explanations are possible.

There are accounts of appearances to various individuals and to small groups. Paul even refers to a group of five hundred, claiming that many of them were still alive when he wrote; but does that really *prove* anything? One can only accept or reject their testimony; for, even granting their sincerity, other explanations are possible.

All of the reported appearances were to disciples. If Jesus really wanted to prove something, why didn't he show himself to Pilate, to Caiaphas, or to the members of the Jewish Sanhedrin? That would have done it! But no, it is not so reported. Always there is this ambiguity about the evidence. When confronted with it, one can believe or one can doubt—or be blind—as these two disciples are blind to the identity of the one who walks beside them now!

Faced with the cruciality of the resurrection, it is not surprising that some later disciples have tried to establish its reality on the grounds of hard facts and irrefutable, empirical evidence. But such efforts are doomed to failure. If there was so much ambiguity about the resurrection of Jesus for those who were closest to him, then the effort twenty centuries later to establish it as a demonstrable fact appears not only futile but also comical!

C. THE ORIGIN AND NATURE OF FAITH IN THE RISEN CHRIST

What then *is* the basis for faith? What is its origin? On what does it depend? The story now moves on to speak to those questions. And what we get now is—of all things—a Bible study!

Chiding them for their blindness to what the prophets had written about the Messiah, the stranger begins to talk with them about the Scriptures: "Was it not necessary that the Christ should suffer these things and enter into his glory?" Then, "beginning with Moses and all of the prophets, he interpreted to them in all the scriptures the things concerning himself."

In one sense these disciples were not ignorant. They knew the facts, but they did not know how to interpret them. They were seeing the suffering and death of the Messiah as a tragedy, as solely an act of wicked men that cut short the promise and the hope. Now they are shown from the Hebrew Scriptures that what has happened in Jerusalem was included in God's plan from the beginning. This was entirely a new idea for them—and too much for them to take in all at once—but already something is happening to them, something they will be able to identify only in the light of another experience.

Anyway, at this point in the story they arrive at Emmaus. They invite the stranger to spend the night with them. He agrees, and the story continues: "And when he was at table with them, he took bread and blessed and broke it, and gave it to them."

Once again the stranger has reversed the roles. On the road he had appeared first as one who had to ask questions about well-known events, and then he became the teacher. Now he is the invited guest who becomes the host; and what begins as a simple evening meal becomes, for Luke's purposes, the sacramental meal—the Lord's Supper!

"And their eyes were opened and they recognized him; and he vanished out of their sight." Even though Jesus immediately vanished from their sight—and this is a very important point in the story—now they know that he is alive and with them. Their sadness is gone, and the dead hope is resurrected! The road that had seemed so long to their weary feet now seems short enough for running all the way back to Jerusalem with the happy news!

IV

Luke has now achieved his purpose. He has shown us where and how Christian faith arises and how it becomes stronger than doubt.

We may not be satisfied with Luke's resolution of the problem—if we really understand what he is saying. We may have hoped for something dramatic and startling, whereas Luke points us to something we may regard as mundane and commonplace.

Luke is not saying that *we* may expect an

experience like that of the Emmaus disciples, that is, an appearance of the risen Christ to our *sight*. He is saying something of a more general nature, namely, *that faith comes through the continuing ministry of the Word and the sacraments.*

By showing us that Jesus vanished from their sight, Luke is reminding us that Jesus is no longer present and accessible as he was in his lifetime or on the road to Emmaus. But he is present and accessible whenever disciples gather to remember him, to interpret the Scriptures, and to break bread as he commanded. The story is suggesting that he is present even when the conversations about him reflect doubts, unbelief, and disappointment; but clearly Luke intends us to see this as the church gathered for worship.

To say this is to say that faith is a gift—the gift of the risen Christ to his church. Faith is not something we can *create* by formulating unassailable doctrinal statements, or by assembling undeniable proofs of the resurrection of Jesus from the dead. It is, rather, *the gift of the presence of the risen Christ;* and that gift is a reality, even though we may for a long time be blind to it because of our slowness of heart.

The promise is that "where two or three are gathered in my name, there am I in the midst of them" (Matt. 18:20). We might wish for something more dramatic than that, something convincing enough to lay to rest our lingering doubts. Nevertheless, in terms of the Emmaus story, Christian faith lives by that experience wherein the absurdity of faith in Jesus is again and again overcome by Christ's own action through the ministry of the Word and the sacraments in the worship of the church.

This is very strange, very strange indeed. Or at least it seems strange in a world so oriented to factual, empirical evidence; but it is verified again and again in Christian experience in all ages.

Faith is a gift! And if it is a gift, then it cannot be bought, earned, constructed by proofs, or conjured up by an act of the will. But if it is a gift, then it can be *sought;* and it is our task to seek it where it is most likely to be found.

PENTECOST

God's Answer to Babel

I

Each one of these stories has a background without which it cannot be understood. The Babel story stands at the conclusion of those introductory chapters of the Bible that portray the human situation in a series of stories. These stories are introduced with a hymn of praise to the goodness of God and his creation. Everything moves in harmony. Man is at peace with God, with himself, and with the created order. But suddenly there is a note of jarring discord. Man is estranged from God, human relationships are strained, and that harmonious relationship with nature is disrupted.

From here on the situation deteriorates rapidly. Cain murders his brother Abel; men invent weapons of destruction and engage in wholesale murder. God wonders if he has made a mistake and decides to wash the whole thing out and start over again, saving only Noah and his family. But Noah himself starts the process all over again, and soon things are just as bad as they were before.

In the last story in this section, men decide to build a great tower for themselves, a tower reaching to the heavens. God has promised that he will never again destroy the earth with a flood, but who knows? They were not willing to settle for that kind of security, so they decide to build their own. But God sees what is being done and he "comes down" and confuses their language. Suddenly they find that they cannot understand each other and the project has to be abandoned. Men are scattered over the face of the earth. Communication and community break down completely.

It is against that background that the biblical narrative begins the long story with which we are all more or less familiar, the story that begins with the call of Abraham and moves across the centuries to the birth, in a stable, of Jesus Christ. During the past six months our worship has been a remembering of his birth, his life, his death, his resurrection, and ascension. And now today we have come to this event and this story about it—Pentecost.

Perhaps it is necessary to make some distinction between the event and the story about it in Acts. It is one of those events that reveals the limitations of human language. Words are always symbols. But in this story they are highly symbolic, and that usage of language must be recognized. The apostles and others present with them experienced the reality and presence of God in a new and different way. The experience itself could be described only in symbolic language. It was "*like* the rush of a mighty wind," and there were "tongues *as of* fire" (italics added).

What happened in that experience can be understood best in terms of its effects. We can never *see* the wind, but we always note its presence and its power by its visible effects on the trees. Even so, the effects of the Spirit on the disciples were clearly perceptible, and here no symbolic language is necessary to describe them. These three effects of the Holy Spirit's coming can be noted: communication was restored; the disciples were empowered to witness to the mighty works of God; and a new community was created. Let us look at these effects in more detail.

The disciples, described in the story as a company of about one hundred twenty persons, were "all filled with the Holy Spirit and began to speak in other tongues, as the Spirit gave them utterance" (Acts 2:4). The story says that people from every nation were present there, and that they were amazed because each one heard the disciples speaking in his own language. Now, what is described here must not be confused with that strange phenomenon Paul is talking about in I Corinthians, the *glossolilia*, or speaking in tongues that correspond to no human language. What happened here was that the disciples were enabled to speak in a language that was foreign to them but native to some of the persons present in their audience. Either that or the miracle was on the hearing side rather than on the speaking side. The point is that the hearers could say, "We hear them telling in our own tongues the mighty works of God" (Acts 2:11).

The disciples were enabled to witness to the mighty works of God, and this was something new. Peter, who heretofore had not exhibited much courage, and who could never get the story straight, suddenly became both bold and eloquent! What a sermon he preached that day! But of course it was not just Peter; it was Peter filled with the Holy Spirit.

At the conclusion of Peter's sermon his hearers asked: "*'What shall we do?'* And Peter said to them, *'Repent, and be baptized every one of you in the name of Jesus Christ for the forgiveness of sins; and you shall receive the gift of the Holy Spirit.'* . . . So those who received his word were baptized, and there were added that day about three thousand souls. And they devoted themselves to the apostle's teaching and fellowship, to the breaking of bread and the prayers" (Acts 2:37-38, 41-42 [italics added]). This was the birth of the Christian community, and that is why we celebrate Pentecost as the birthday of the church.

II

So that is what Pentecost meant. But what *does* it mean? How do we understand and appropriate the inner meaning of this event for our lives today?

We need the Babel story as background for understanding the inner meaning of the Pentecost story. The Babel story attempts to explain why communication is so difficult, not only between nations and cultures, but also between individuals who occupy the same territory and share a common culture—not only between strangers, but also between those who live under the same roof. Once in some far-off mythical time, when men lived in harmony with their creator, the world had one language and people could really communicate. But when man is unwilling to trust God and seeks to establish his own security, then his words become weapons, weapons used to defend himself against both God and his neighbor. The result of this double alienation is the disintegration of the orders of life. All the orders of life are affected at all levels—international, national, local community, family. The Babel story expresses the biblical verdict on all secular civilizations. When the center of life is that which man constructs in his pride, in an effort to establish his own security and autonomy, then confusion comes upon us and we are threatened with chaos.

In the Pentecost story, God once again "comes down," but this time for a different purpose. This time he comes, not to scatter men abroad and confuse their language, but to give them a new language and bind them together in a new community. The Holy Spirit comes into the hearts and minds of those who hear the gospel. They find that they are reconciled to God, and then they begin to hear and understand one another—even across the barriers of different cultures and ancient hostilities. So Pentecost is nothing less than the Babel story in reverse. It represents the experience of God's grace creating the spirit of peace and unity.

III

"Well," you might be saying to yourself, "that wraps it all up very neatly. And of course it is a lovely thought—but where have you been living recently? In some kind of a dream world? Life as I experience it still seems to fit the Babel story far better than the Pentecost story. And [you might want to add] I am not thinking only of the world here. I am thinking about the church, too. Just look at the way Christians are divided into different denominations, not to mention the disssensions and strife that exist within each denomination. Or, bring it down to the local congregation, and just ask yourself how much real unity and peace and reconciliation you can find there."

If that is what you are saying to yourself, then let me say, "Yes, I know what you mean. I know very well that Babel is a fact of our existence, even in the church." But having said that, I would want to go on and say that Pentecost is also a reality of our present existence. *Both* of these stories describe the present realities of our situation. We must not understand them as if they describe our situation in some neatly divided "before and after" fashion—like a television commercial about using the right toothpaste. The spirit of Babel is very much with us, even in the church; but so also is the spirit of Pentecost. That is the way we experience life, isn't it? As Christians we are forgiven sinners—but sinners still. We are reconciled to God an to one another, but we still experience some of the old alienation. Indeed, we are always moving somewhere between alienation and reconciliation. We are always moving somewhere between Babel and Pentecost, with each of these mighty forces contending for the mastery of our lives.

If ever a man felt the fury of Babel, in a church that showed little evidence of the Spirit, that man was Dietrich Bonhoeffer. Yet on a certain Pentecost Sunday he wrote from his prison a letter to his parents that contained these words: "At the tower of Babel all the tongues were confounded and as a result men could no longer understand one another. . . . This confusion is now brought to an end by the language of God, which is universally intelligible and the only means of communication among men. And the church is the place where the miracle happens."

The church is the place where the miracle happens? Such faith may be too much for us in terms of what we see today in the Church, but we must not act as if Pentecost never happened. It did happen. God poured out his Spirit on the church to create something new in this world. And the gift of the Spirit was an *enduring* gift. The church has been sometimes more and sometimes less receptive to the Spirit, but it has never been wholly without the Spirit. If this were not so, the spirit of Babel would have overwhelmed us long ago.

The church may not appear to be a very great hope, but perhaps it is the last, best hope of the world. Says George A. Buttrick: "The New Pentecost cannot come without the *Church*, a new Church in every age, yet always springing from the old Church, as the old Church sprang from the Christ-Event, whose Spirit is ever new because Eternal; the Church always blundering in human pride and always redeemed as being the Body of Christ" *(Sermons Preached in a University Church* [Nashville: Abingdon Press, 1959], p. 201).

If we are threatened with a new outbreak of Babel in our times we are also encouraged to hope for a new outpouring of God's Spirit. And we are called to live in that hope—the hope that God will bless us with a fresh outpouring of his Spirit to cleanse, renew, and empower the church for its witness to the mighty works of God.

IV

We are called to "wait for the Spirit," but we must learn to wait as those first disciples waited. They were men of prayer, and that is important to note. But it is equally important to note that they were men under orders. Jesus had told them to wait in Jerusalem for the promised coming of the Spirit. And he had said: "You shall receive power when the Holy Spirit has come upon you; and you shall be my witnesses in Jerusalem and in all Judea and Samaria and to the end of the earth" (Acts 1:8).

So they were men under orders. They were where Jesus told them to be. And they were ready to move when the Spirit said to move!

There is a certain *economy* of the Spirit that must be recognized. The Spirit is not given promiscuously. The Spirit is not given for our personal ecstasy. *The Spirit is given to empower the church for mission.*

Our mission is to proclaim in words and in deeds the wonderful works of God, so that all people everywhere may hear and be reconciled to God and to one another. The new Pentecost will come when we are actually ready and willing to undertake that mission—not halfheartedly, and not with the bits and scraps of our lives, but with our whole being.

Old Testament Lesson: Deuteronomy 6:1-15
New Testament Lesson: Ephesians 4:1-8, 25-32

TRINITY SUNDAY

Theology and Experience

I

The announcement that we are celebrating Trinity Sunday today will not necessarily create a ripple of excitement and anticipation in the congregation. Indeed, I must confess that I am often tempted to pass over this Sunday with no mention of it. It poses something of a problem for those who want to celebrate the Christian Year. The problem is that Trinity Sunday, unlike the other great festival days on the church calendar, commemorates an idea rather than an event.

Advent and Christmas, Good Friday, Easter, and Pentecost all focus on events—events that can be imagined and that have been portrayed in countless works of art. But how do we go about celebrating an idea—especially one so complicated and confusing as the concept of the Trinity, with its "three in one" and "one in three" jargon?

Perhaps we should not even try! I suspect that

a good many Christians in the church today would applaud that suggestion. Some have been quite vocal in their impatience with the whole trinitarian concept, and they have their reasons. They point out that the doctrine of the Trinity was not accepted officially in the church until the fourth century and that it does not even appear in the Scriptures. They attribute its existence entirely to a few theologians, and theologians, as everyone knows, love to take simple matters and make them dreadfully complicated! And so they suggest, "Why not dispense with this difficult doctrine?"

II

Why not, indeed? The suggestion is superficially appealing, but I can think of at least two reasons why we should not go along with it. *First, because the doctrine of the Trinity is continually present in the worship of the Church.* We invoke the presence of the Father, the Son, and the Holy Spirit in most of our prayers. We sing the Gloria Patri—"Glory be to the Father, and to the Son, and to the Holy Ghost." We sing the traditional doxology—"Praise God from whom all blessings flow. . . . Praise Father, Son, and Holy Ghost." Most church services close with Paul's trinitarian benediction: "The grace of the

Lord Jesus Christ and the love of God and the fellowship of the Holy Spirit be with you all" (II Cor. 13:14). We always offer the sacrament of baptism in the name of the Father, the Son, and the Holy Spirit. Further, there are references to the Trinity in many of the hymns the church uses regularly in its worship.

Now, since that is the case, dispensing with the doctrine of the Trinity is not so simple a matter as it at first appears to be. A better approach might be that of occasionally talking about what we mean by this language, difficult though that task may be.

But there is a *second* reason why we cannot afford to dispense with the doctrine of the Trinity: *it incorporates something which is absolutely essential to the Christian faith.*

Unitarianism has been on the scene for a long time. It is in fact older than the Christian faith, and it is still around as a live option. To say—as it does—that there is one God and that Jesus Christ was simply a great teacher, perhaps the greatest of all the prophets, seems so reasonable that we might wonder why this interpretation has not captured the field. It may be, of course, that many Christians in the orthodox churches are actually unitarian in their personal beliefs, but that is a matter of speculation; and the church as a whole is certainly not moving in that direction in its theology. Perhaps we should wonder why this is so. Why is it that the vast majority of Christians in all ages have rejected the simpler answer of unitarianism and continued to affirm the complex creed of trinitarianism? The answer, I suggest, is that *unitarianism simply is not big enough to fit the facts of Christian experience!*

III

On further reflection I am not so sure that it is correct to say that Trinity Sunday commemorates an idea rather than an event. Perhaps we will be more accurate if we say that *it commemorates and enshrines the church's experienced reality of God as Father, Son, and Holy Spirit.*

What we sometimes forget is that experience *precedes* theology. Experienced reality is the building blocks out of which the house of doctrine is built. Theology is reflection on experience and the attempt to understand and give an ordered expression to the experience. (Incidentally, this may explain why theology is boring and confusing to some people. If theology is a matter of wrestling with an experience we have never had, then how can it be anything other than boring and confusing?)

It is true that the doctrine of the Trinity was not formulated until the fourth century; but it is also true that its formulation at that time did not stem either from the desire to give a metaphysical definition of God or from some newly acquired revelation. The intention was simply to attempt to recognize and express *what had been the Christian community's experience of God from the very beginning*. The doctrine grew naturally out of two facts with which the community had been confronted—the fact of Jesus Christ and the fact of the Holy Spirit. Let us see how this came about.

IV

We must remember that all of those in the primitive church were steeped in the tradition of monotheism. The first article of faith in the religion of Israel was: "Hear, O Israel: The Lord our God is one Lord" (Deut. 6:4). Amidst the confusion of many gods in the other nations, the prophets of Israel stood up and in the name of Yahweh cried: "Turn to me and be saved, all the ends of the earth! For I am God, and there is no other" (Isa. 45:22).

For us, monotheism is so natural that we don't even think about another possibility, but in the ancient world it was something unique, the good news that there is not a pantheon of powers but one God who is the lord of all.

Now, this doctrine of the one God was deeply embedded in those first disciples of Jesus. And they were the ones who had to wrestle with the meaning of Jesus. There was a mystery about him of which they were conscious even in the days of his bodily presence, and his influence on them was even stronger after he was gone from their sight. Who was he? They were faced with the task of answering that question for themselves, and the answer had to be large enough to fit the facts of their experience. From the moment he had come into their lives, everything had been different. Ever since they had known him, they had known God in a different way.

How could they account for all this? They were forced—these strong monotheists—to say things that suggested that in their dealings with Jesus they were somehow dealing with God. But did this mean that Jesus and God were identical? No—for the reality of Jesus' humanity could not be denied. The disciples knew very well that Jesus had been tempted; they had seen him hungry and tired; they had seen him suffer and die. They found, further, that they could not do justice to their experience by saying that Jesus was a kind of demigod, half god and half man. And so they were forced to say things about God that had never been said before by any good Jew, things that before they met Jesus they themselves would have regarded as blasphemous! They began speaking of God as "the Father" and "the Son." Although they did not attempt to explain this or to work out all the implications of it, they found that it was the natural, even the necessary way to talk about God.

But there was something else that happened that made the doctrine of the Trinity necessary—even though it would not be stated formally until many years had passed. And that was the experience of Pentecost.

Jesus, in the days of his flesh, had made them feel the presence of God. Then he had gone away. But then there was the experience of the Holy Spirit at Pentecost, after which they were surprised to find that God was present in their lives in a way that was even more real and powerful than had been true when Jesus was visibly present with them. What did this mean? It was a new way of experiencing God's presence; yet in another way it was not a new thing, since it heightened their sense of the one God they had always known, and known most recently in Jesus. They soon found themselves talking about the Holy Spirit as if he were God also!

We have only to open the New Testament and read, to confirm the fact that the writers used language that refers to God as the Father, the Son, and the Holy Spirit. Therefore, it is not altogether accurate to say that the doctrine of the Trinity is not found in the New Testament. It is true that it is not there in the form of doctrine, but the *experience* of the Trinity is there, the experience that made necessary the formulation of the doctrine if Christians were going to tell the world what they believed about God.

V

Now, all of this may throw some light on why and how this doctrine came to be, and it may remove some of the objections to it. It leaves unanswered the principal objection, which may be stated as follows: Granted the reality of the experience, why is it necessary to attempt any explanation of it—especially since the attempts have come off so poorly?

Let me speak to that question by saying something about the purpose served by the doctrine of the Trinity. We can understand that purpose better if we understand the purpose of theology in general. Theology has a limited aim. Its aim is not that of trying to *explain* the mystery of God, not that of trying to capture the meaning of God in some words and formulas. It does not even intend, in most instances, to give answers. Its aim is rather that of pointing towards the fullness of the truth about God. Its aim is to leave room for the fullness of truth by rejecting some answers that are too small.

I think it is helpful to us to remember that intention of theology and the church, especially when we look at this doctrine of the Trinity. This is *not* an instance of the church saying, "Look, we have come up with an explanation of the mystery of God!" The doctrine of the Trinity does not explain God, nor was it meant to do so. It was meant, rather, to preserve the mystery of God's revelation of himself from answers that are too small. It was meant to protect the fullness of Christian experience from all interpretations that would leave out or deny some of its vital parts.

It is only in this context that we should regard the doctrine as answers to questions, which in one sense it is. It is an attempt to answer some questions about the nature of God as God has revealed himself. It speaks to the question "Who *is* God?" And what we have to recognize is that the word "God" is an essentially meaningless word! The word itself is simply a vessel into which the contents are poured, and the contents may vary considerably from one person to another, from one religion to another. The statement "I believe in God" tells us nothing at all about the faith of the person making such a statement. The question remains, "God who?" The doctrine of the Trinity speaks forthrightly to that question; moreover, Shirley Guthrie contends, "it is the uniquely Christian answer to the question who God is, the answer which distinguishes the Christian understanding of God from that of other religious or philosophical views" (*Christian Doctrine* [Richmond: John Knox Press, 1969], p. 89).

VI

Finally, I mentioned earlier that the Trinity appears in the experience and worship of the church long before it appears as a doctrinal statement. The New Testament abounds with references to God as Father, as Son, and as Holy Spirit, and so also does the liturgy of the early church. The worship of the church expressed not merely what some theologians presumed to be true but what ordinary Christians knew to be true in their own experience of God. They were saying, suggests George Hendry, "In Christ we have God *with* us, and in the Holy Spirit we have God *in* us, without his ever ceasing to be God *over* us" (*The Westminster Confession for Today* [Richmond: John Knox Press, 1960], p. 43).

That is a significant fact for us to note; for I am sure that it is much easier for us to deal with our own experience of God as Father, Son, and Holy Spirit than it is to cope with the doctrine of the

Trinity. This does not mean that we can dispense with the doctrine. It serves a good and necessary purpose; nevertheless, it is the experience itself that gives the doctrine meaning.

This is most fortunate; for insofar as we are Christians at all, it is because of what God has done for us and in us as Father, Son, and Holy Spirit. In the words of Donald Baillie, "The God who was incarnate in Christ dwells in us through the Holy Spirit; and that is the secret of the Christian life."

That is the experience the doctrine of the Trinity seeks to recognize and preserve!